Book Three

Pieces to Play

with

Step by Step

by

Edna Mae Burnam

To my grandchildren

CONTENTS

Book
ISBN 978-1-4234-3596-9

Book/CD
ISBN 978-1-4234-3613-3

WILLIS MUSIC

EXCLUSIVELY DISTRIBUTED BY

HAL•LEONARD®
CORPORATION
7777 W. BLUEMOUND RD. P.O. BOX 13819 MILWAUKEE, WI 53213

Visit Hal Leonard Online at
www.halleonard.com

TO THE TEACHER

The pieces in this book have been composed to correlate exactly with the Edna Mae Burnam Piano Course STEP BY STEP—Book Three. Prefixed to each piece is an indication of the exact page of STEP BY STEP—Book Three at which a selection from PIECES TO PLAY may be introduced. When the student reaches this page, he/she is ready to play with ease and understanding.

All of the pieces in this book may serve as repertoire for the student at this level.

The pieces in this book should be:

1. Perfected;
2. Memorized;
3. Played with expression and poise;
4. Kept in readiness to play for company.

Edna Mae Burnam

The student is ready to play this piece when he has reached page 9 of
Edna Mae Burnam's STEP BY STEP - Book Three.

CLOUDS, RAIN AND RAINBOW

By EDNA MAE BURNAM

Clouds

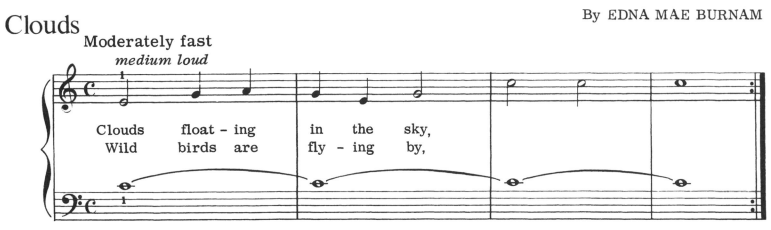

Clouds float – ing in the sky,
Wild birds are fly – ing by,

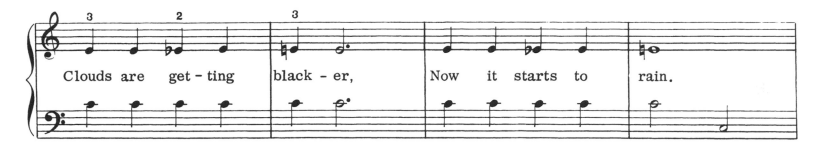

Clouds are get – ting black – er, Now it starts to rain.

Rain

Rainbow

Smoothly

TWO RIDES ON A MERRY-GO-ROUND

By EDNA MAE BURNAM

Getting Tickets

First time playing – Getting ticket for first ride.
On repeat   – Getting ticket for second ride.

Rides

Merrily

First time playing – First ride.
On repeat   – Second ride.

The student is ready to play this piece when he has reached page 19 of Edna Mae Burnam's STEP BY STEP – Book Three.

LITTLE SPIDER SPINS A WEB

By EDNA MAE BURNAM

Moderately fast

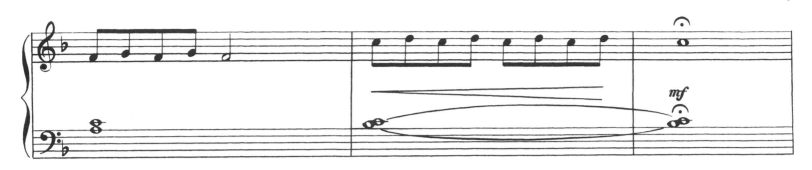

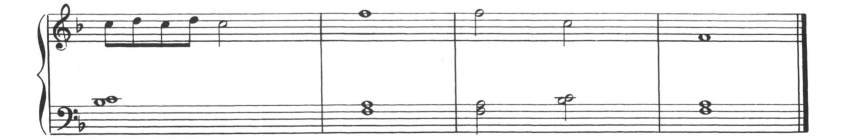

The student is ready to play this piece when he has reached page 26 of
Edna Mae Burnam's STEP BY STEP - Book Three.

THE STOP-AND-GO DONKEY

By EDNA MAE BURNAM

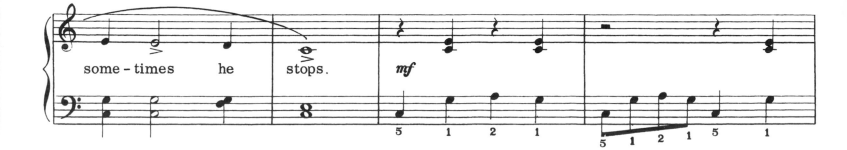

mp There's a

lit — tle don-key go—ing down the road, But some—times he

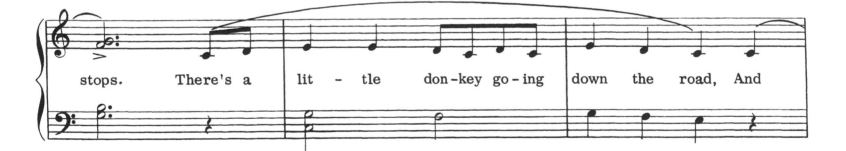

stops. There's a lit — tle don-key go—ing down the road, And

some — times he stops, f some—times he stops.

*The student is ready to play this piece when he has reached page 34 of
Edna Mae Burnam's STEP BY STEP – Book Three.*

THE CAVE IS DEEP

By EDNA MAE BURNAM

Rather slow

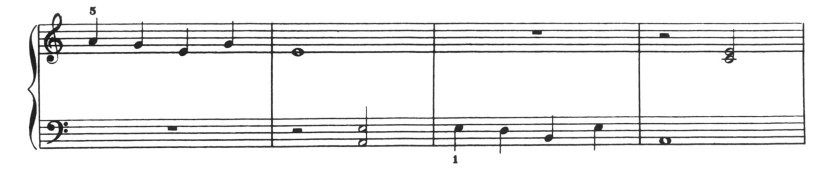

The student is ready to play this piece when he has reached page 39 of
Edna Mae Burnam's STEP BY STEP – Book Three.

SINGING THOUGHTS

By EDNA MAE BURNAM

In a singing style

IN A DEPARTMENT STORE

By EDNA MAE BURNAM

March-like

On the first floor – Buying shoes.

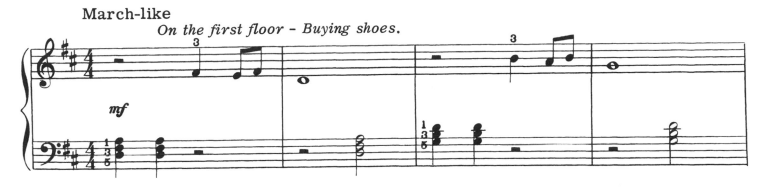

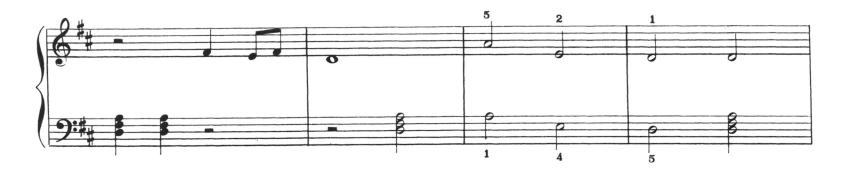

Going up to the second floor.

Happy and light

On the second floor - Buying toys.

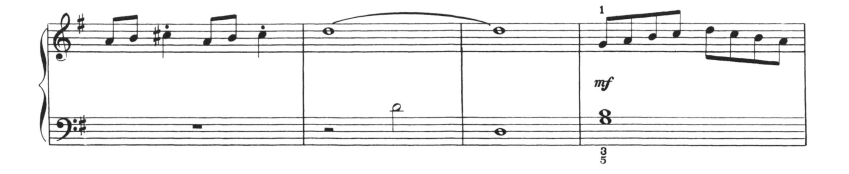

The student is ready to play this piece when he has reached page 45 of
Edna Mae Burnam's STEP BY STEP – Book Three.

SONG OF THE WINDMILL

By EDNA MAE BURNAM

Certificate of Merit

This is to certify that

_____

has successfully completed

PIECES TO PLAY

BOOK THREE
BY
EDNA MAE BURNAM

and is now eligible for promotion to

PIECES TO PLAY

BOOK FOUR

_____Teacher

Date _____

Edna Mae Burnam

Edna Mae Burnam (1907–2007) is one of the most respected names in piano pedagogy. She began her study of the instrument at age seven with lessons from her mother, and went on to major in piano at the University of Washington and Chico State Teacher's College in Los Angeles. In 1935, she sold "The Clock That Stopped"—one of her original compositions still in print today—to a publisher for $20. In 1937, Burnam began her long and productive association with Florence, Kentucky-based Willis Music, who signed her to her first royalty contract. In 1950, she sent manuscripts to Willis for an innovative piano series comprised of short and concise warm-up exercises—she drew stick figures indicating where the "real" illustrations should be dropped in. That manuscript, along with the original stick figures, became the best-selling *A Dozen a Day* series, which has sold more than 25 million copies worldwide; the stick-figure drawings are now icons.

Burnam followed up on the success of *A Dozen a Day* with her *Step by Step Piano Course*. This method teaches students the rudiments of music in a logical order and manageable pace, for gradual and steady progress. She also composed hundreds of individual songs and pieces, many based on whimsical subjects or her international travels. These simple, yet effective learning tools for children studying piano have retained all their charm and unique qualities, and remain in print today in the Willis catalog. Visit **www.halleonard.com** to browse all available piano music by Edna Mae Burnam.

A DOZEN A DAY
by Edna Mae Burnam

The **Dozen a Day** books are universally recognized as one of the most remarkable technique series on the market for all ages! Each book in this series contains short warm-up exercises to be played at the beginning of each practice session, providing excellent day-to-day training for the student. The audio CD is playable on any CD player and features fabulous backing tracks by Ric Iannone. For Windows® and Mac computer users, the CD is enhanced so you can access MIDI files for each exercise and adjust the tempo.

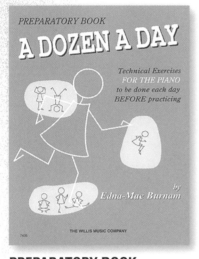

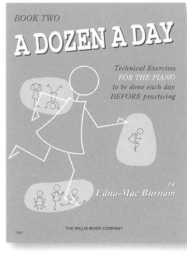

PREPARATORY BOOK
00414222	Book Only	$3.95
00406476	Book/CD Pack	$8.95
00406479	CD Only	$9.95
00406477	Book/GM Disk Pack	$13.95
00406480	GM Disk Only	$9.95

BOOK 1
00413366	Book Only	$3.95
00406481	Book/CD Pack	$8.95
00406483	CD Only	$9.95
00406482	Book/GM Disk Pack	$13.90
00406484	GM Disk Only	$9.95

BOOK 2
00413826	Book Only	$3.95
00406485	Book/CD Pack	$8.95
00406487	CD Only	$9.95
00406486	Book/GM Disk Pack	$13.90
00406488	GM Disk Only	$9.95

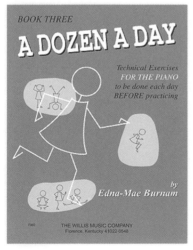

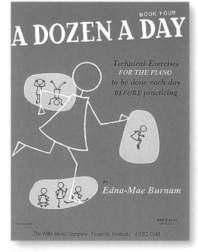

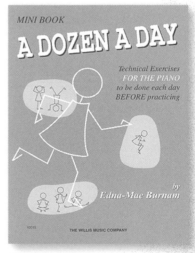

BOOK 3
00414136	Book Only	$4.95
00416760	Book/CD Pack	$9.95

BOOK 4
00415686	Book Only	$5.95
00416761	Book/CD Pack	$10.95

MINI BOOK
00404073	Mini Book	$3.95
00406472	Book/CD Pack	$8.95
00406474	CD Only	$9.95
00406473	Book/GM Disk Pack	$13.90
00406475	GM Disk Only	$9.95

WM WILLIS MUSIC

EXCLUSIVELY DISTRIBUTED BY
HAL•LEONARD®

Prices, contents, and availability subject to change without notice. Prices listed in U.S. funds.